ULTIMATE GUITAR PLAY-ALONG

BOOK & PLAY-ALONG CDs
WITH **TNT** TONE 'N' TEMPO CHANGER

LED ZEPP

G000166291

Play Along with 8 Great-Sounding Tracks

About the TNT Changer

Use the TNT software to change keys, loop playback, and mute tracks for play-along. For complete instructions, see the *TnT ReadMe.pdf* file on your enhanced CDs.

Windows users: insert a CD into your computer, double-click on My Computer, right-click on your CD drive icon, and select Explore to locate the file.

Mac users: insert a CD into your computer and double-click on the CD icon on your desktop to locate the file.

Produced by
Alfred Music Publishing Co., Inc.
P.O. Box 10003
Van Nuys, CA 91410-0003
alfred.com

Printed in USA.

ISBN-10: 0-7390-5946-7 (Book & 2 CDs)
ISBN-13: 978-0-7390-5946-3 (Book & 2 CDs)

Cover photo: © Bob Gruen

Alfred Cares. Contents printed on 100% recycled paper.

LED ZEPPELIN

Contents

EDITOR'S NOTE

It is simply impossible to actually recreate the recorded performances of Led Zeppelin and the production techniques of Jimmy Page. The intention of these recordings is to aid in the study of the guitar parts by providing credible backing tracks to play along with, hopefully capturing the spirit of the original music. Ultimately, it is essential to listen to, and try and emulate, the original Led Zeppelin tracks to really understand the musical nuance, intensity, and brilliance of those recordings.

CREDITS

Supervisory editors: Brad Tolinski and Jimmy Brown
Project manager and music editor: Tom Farncombe
Audio recording and mixing: Jonas Persson
Guitars and guitar transcriptions: Arthur Dick
Additional transcription and editing: Jimmy Brown
Bass guitar and bass transcriptions: Paul Townsend
Drums, percussion, and drum transcriptions: Noam Lederman
Keyboards and keyboard transcriptions: Paul Honey
Music engraving: Paul Ewers Music Design
Thanks to Chandler Guitars (www.chandlerguitars.co.uk).

Special thanks to Mark Lodge at Hiwatt UK for supplying the Hiwatt 100 Head, an exact replica of Jimmy Page's amp from the Led Zeppelin sessions. **HIWATT**
WWW.HIWATT.CO.UK

EQUIPMENT LIST

In addition to the instruments specified under Recording Notes (starting on page 4), the following were used for the recordings:

1968 Ludwig drum kit (24" bass drum, 13" rack tom, 16" floor tom, 18" second floor tom)
Paiste cymbals
1991 Fender Jazz Bass
1978 Fender Precision Bass
1962 reissue Fender Jazz Bass (strung with flatwound strings)
Ashdown bass amplification
Miscellaneous guitar effects:
    Fulltone Full-Drive 2
    Pete Cornish sustain pedal
    Celmo Sardine Can compressor
    Jim Dunlop Crybaby wah-wah pedal

Recording Notes

The following notes detail the guitars and amplifiers used on each song in this book, as an indication of how one might try to match the kind of tone Jimmy Page achieved on the original Led Zeppelin recordings. These choices were based on the information available about the original recording setups. However, with other, less-controllable factors to consider (studio size, mic type and placement, location, tape machines, and recording consoles), choices about the right sound were driven as much by ear as by the reported original conditions.

Black Dog

The rhythm parts for this song were played on a 1959 Les Paul. This was recorded direct using a Universal Audio DI through a Tube-Tech CL 1B valve compressor, overdriving the input on a Manley valve EQ before feeding the signal back into Pro Tools.

The solo was played on a 1969 Telecaster using a Hiwatt 100, a Fender 2x12 cab, and rotary speaker effects from a Line 6 MM4 modulation pedal.

Communication Breakdown

The main riffs were played on a 1972 Fender Telecaster through a Cornell Romany 10 watt amplifier and a 1964 Watkins Electronics Westminster 5 watt combo. This combination was intended to capture the tone of Jimmy Page's Supro amps.

The other rhythm parts were played on the 1972 Tele through the Hiwatt 100 amp. The solo was recorded using the 1969 Telecaster and the Hiwatt.

The organ parts were played on a Nord Electro 2 modelling keyboard, recorded through a 1965 VOX AC30.

Dazed and Confused

The main parts were tracked on the 1959 Gibson Les Paul through the Hiwatt 100; the higher parts were recorded with the same guitar through the Cornell combo.

The reverb for the solo sections (played with a violin bow, of course!) is from a Lexicon PCM91.

Heartbreaker

The two guitars for the main sections were the 1969 Telecaster and a 1952 Les Paul, both recorded through the Hiwatt. The solo was played with the 1959 Les Paul.

Immigrant Song

All the parts were tracked using the 1952 Les Paul and the Hiwatt. The tremolo parts were played through the Fender 2x12 cab with a Roger Mayer Voodoo Vibe + vibrato unit.

Rock and Roll

The rhythm guitars on this recording are the 1952 Les Paul played through the Hiwatt and Cornell, and a 1969 Les Paul Black Beauty through the Cornell and the WEM Westminster combo.

The harmony parts were tracked using the 1969 Telecaster through the Hiwatt and Cornell amps; the solo was on the same guitar, but using a Marshall JCM2000.

Since I've Been Loving You

The main parts for this were played on the 1952 Les Paul through a combination of the Hiwatt and Watkins amps.

The solo was played on the 1959 Les Paul through the Marshall and the Cornell.

The organ parts were recorded with the Nord Electro 2.

On the original recording, John Paul Jones's bass line was played on the pedals of his Hammond organ; this was recreated here on a Fender Jazz Bass with flatwound strings.

Whole Lotta Love

The main parts were played on a 1952 Goldtop Les Paul reissue through the Hiwatt 100. The panning sliding part in the chorus was recorded as an ascending slide and then reversed and put through an Eventide flanger.

The solo breaks were played on the 1959 Les Paul using a Roger Mayer Treble Booster through the Marshall JCM2000 with a 4x12 cab; this was then overdriven through a Studer A80 tape machine.

Bongos and cymbals were overdubbed for the middle section alongside tape-effected guitar.

BLACK DOG

Words and Music by
JIMMY PAGE, ROBERT PLANT
and JOHN PAUL JONES

Freely (♩ = 82)

Verse

(4.) I got to roll, can't stand still, got a flam-ing heart, can't get my fill.

Gtr. 2 drum cue: Gtrs. 1+2

(Gtr. 1 plays open A5 chord as before)

Freely

5. Eyes that shine, burn-ing red,__ dreams of you__ all through my head.

drum cue:

(♩ = 82)

Ah ah, ah ah

ah ah, ah ah, ah ah, ah ah, ah._____

drum cue:

Hey, ba-by, oh, ba-by, pret-ty ba-by, dar-ling can't you do me now?
ba-by, oh, ba-by, pret-ty ba-by, move me while you do me now.

*The metre of this song is somewhat controversial, especially in the **Chorus** and **Solo** sections.
Previous editions suggest that the kick drum indicates the downbeat, meaning irregular bars at certain points.
However, the drum clicks and cues before these sections would make it seem that the metre actually remains constant, in 4/4;
therefore the snare drum remains on the backbeat throughout. This is reflected in this arrangement.*

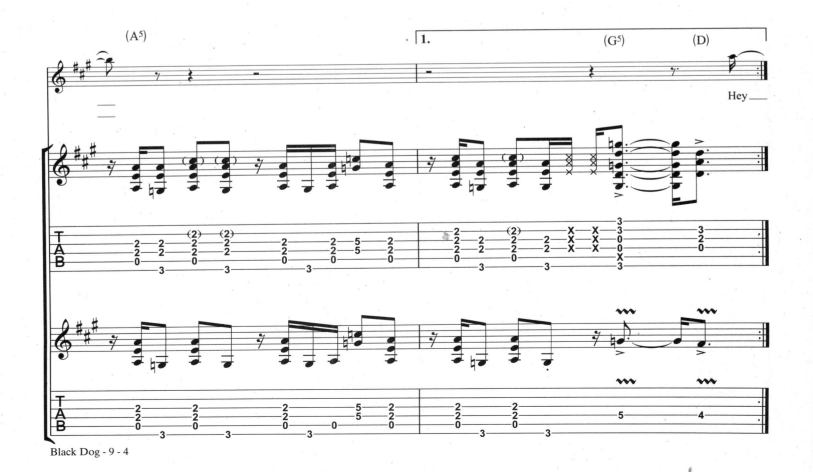

Hey

9. All I ask___ for, all I pray,___ stead - y - roll -ing wo-man gon - na come my way.___
10. Need a woman gonna hold my hand, won't tell me no lies, make me a hap - py man.___

Ah ah, ah ah, ah ah, ah ah, ah ah, ah ah, ah.

Black Dog - 9 - 8

COMMUNICATION BREAKDOWN

Words and Music by
JIMMY PAGE, JOHN PAUL JONES and JOHN BONHAM

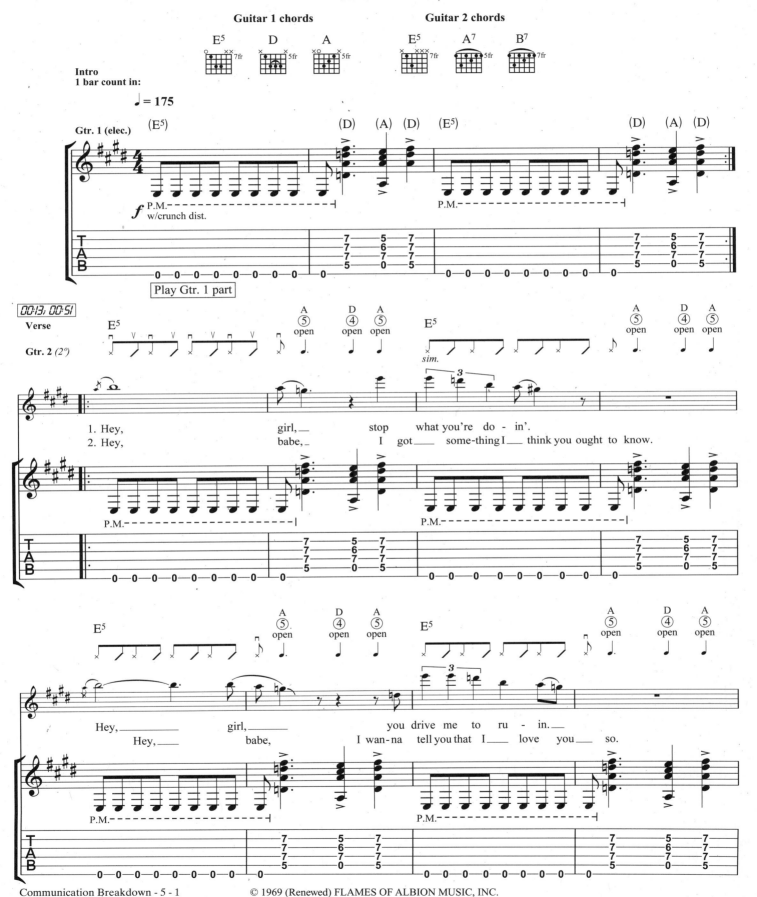

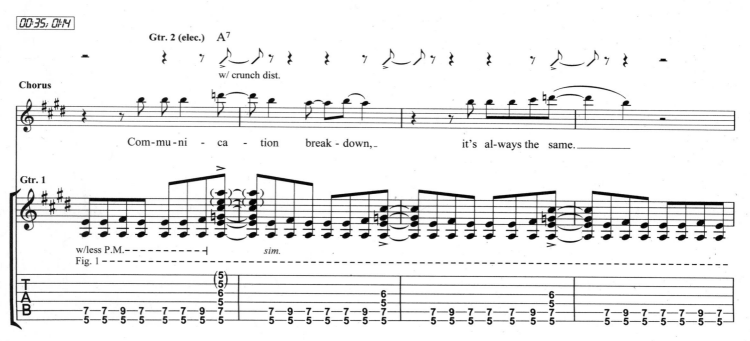

I don't know what it is that I like a-bout you, but I like it a lot. Won't

I wan-na hold you in my arms, yeah.

you let me hold you, let me feel your lov-ing touch?

I'm nev-er gon-na let you go 'cause I like your charms.

00:35; 01:14

Gtr. 2 (elec.) A⁷

w/ crunch dist.

Chorus

Com-mu-ni-ca-tion break-down, it's al-ways the same.

Gtr. 1

w/less P.M.
sim.
Fig. 1

Communication Breakdown - 5 - 5

DAZED AND CONFUSED

Words and Music by
JIMMY PAGE

Dazed and Confused - 11 - 1

Dazed and Confused - 11 - 2

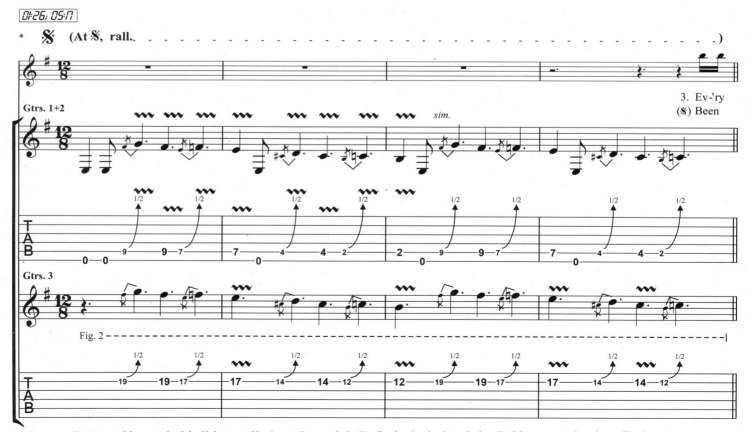

*The original versions of this song by Jake Holmes, and by Jimmy Page with the Yardbirds, clearly place the low E of the signature bass line riff on beat 1 and the high G on beat 1. In the first 2 verses John Bonham chooses to turn the metre around, placing the high G on beat 2. From this point on he clearly turns the metre around again, placing the high G on beat 2 as in the original versions. He remains in this metre for the rest of the song. All subsequent versions of this song follow this exact same pattern of turning the metre around.

Dazed and Confused - 11 - 4

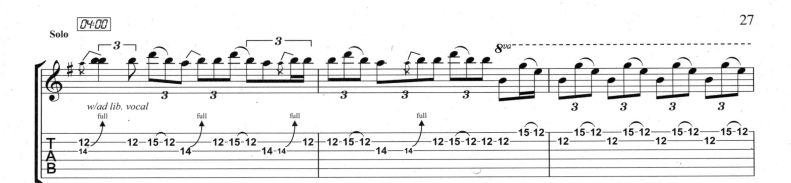

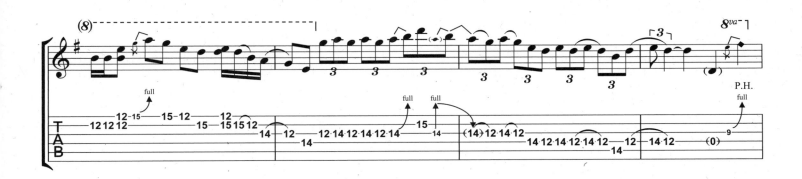

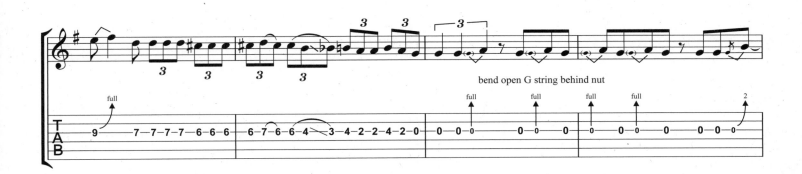

Dazed and Confused - 11 - 8

Dazed and Confused - 11 - 9

Dazed and Confused - 11 - 10

Dazed and Confused - 11 - 11

HEARTBREAKER

Words and Music by
JIMMY PAGE, ROBERT PLANT,
JOHN PAUL JONES and JOHN BONHAM

Intro
1 bar count in:

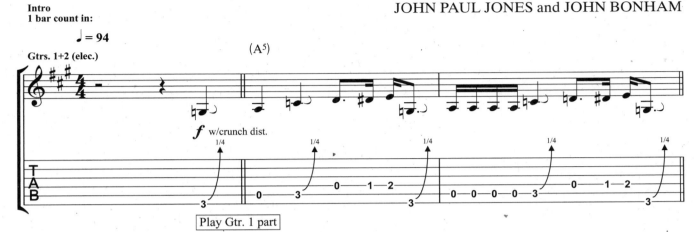

Play Gtr. 1 part

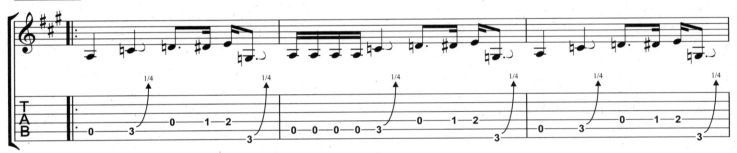

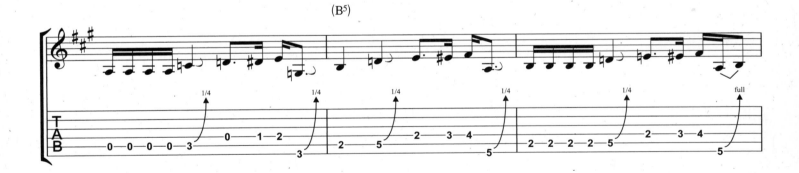

2. Well, it's

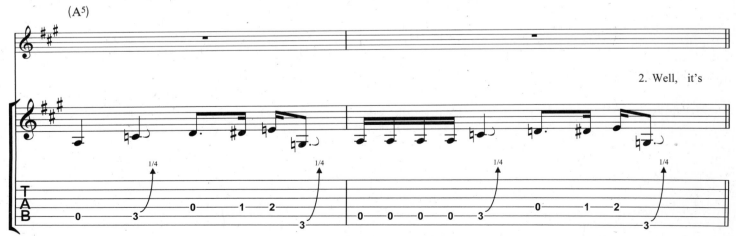

Heartbreaker - 9 - 1

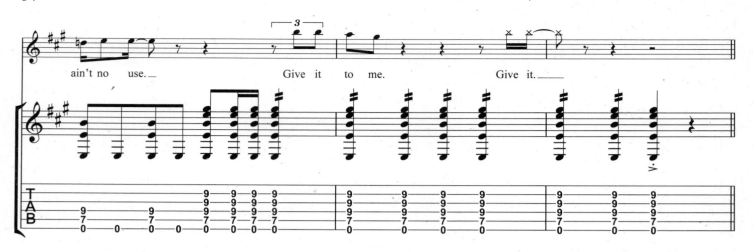

ain't no use.___ Give it to me. Give it.___

`02:10`
Interlude

Freely

Gtr. 3 (elec.)*

f Gtr. 3 w/dist.
Gtrs. 1+2 tacet

bend string
behind nut

Play Gtr. 3 part

*The unaccompanied guitar solo on the original recording sounds 1/4 tone sharp of concert pitch (pitch returns to normal when Gtrs. 1+2 re-enter).

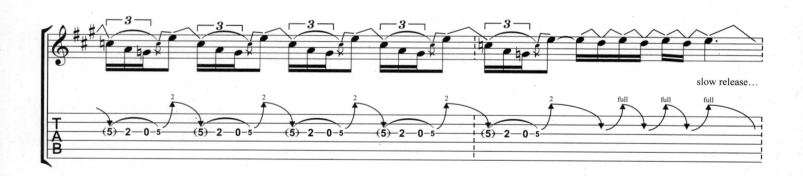

slow release...

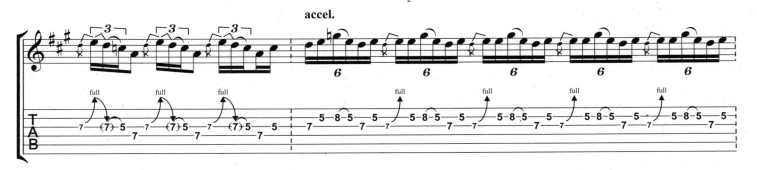

Heartbreaker - 9 - 5

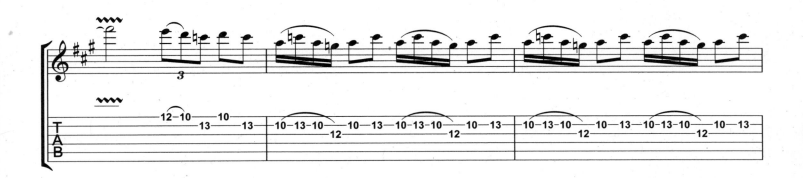

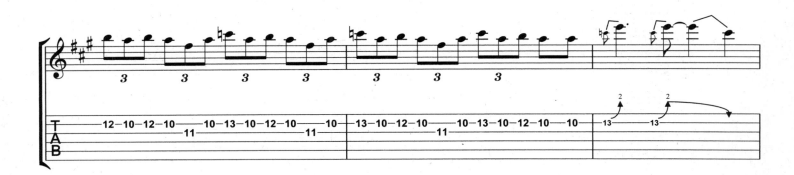

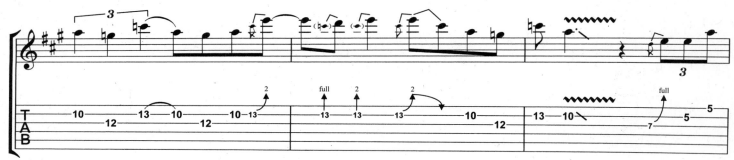

Heartbreaker - 9 - 7

Heartbreaker - 9 - 9

IMMIGRANT SONG

Words and Music by
JIMMY PAGE and ROBERT PLANT

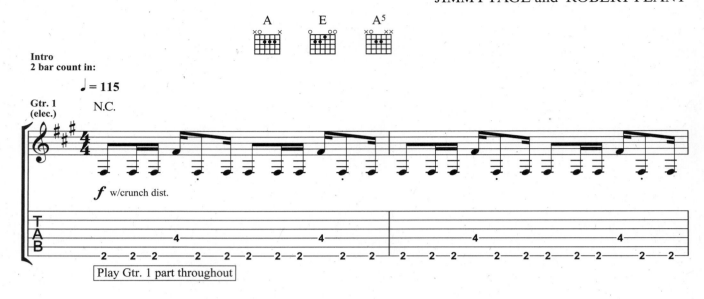

Immigrant Song - 5 - 1

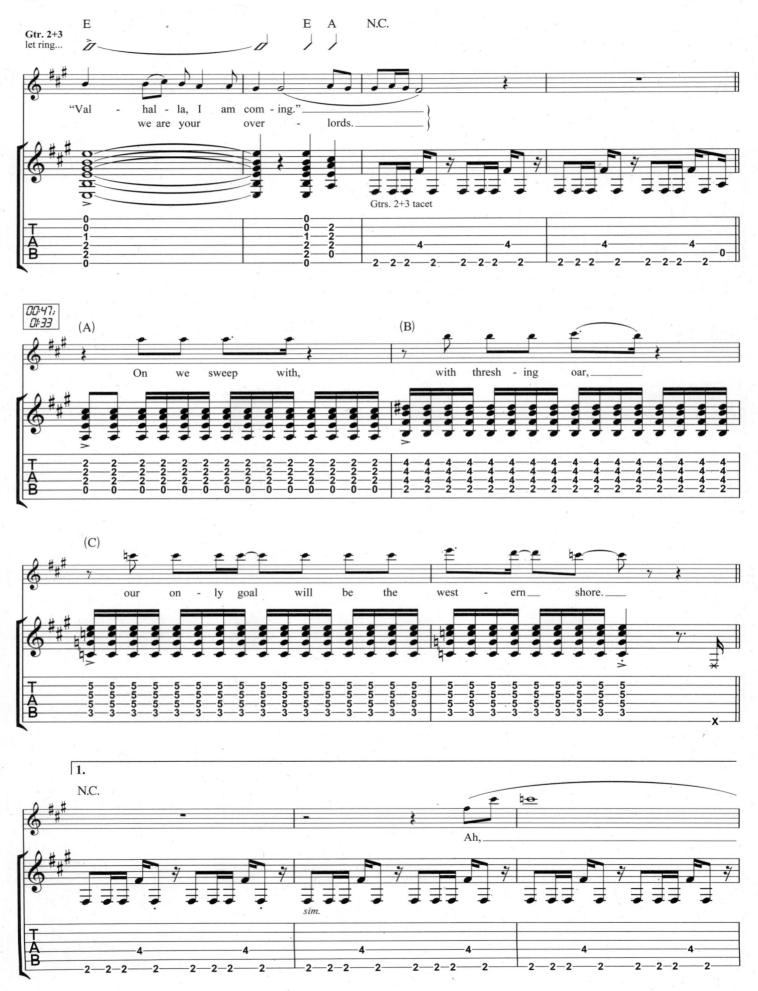

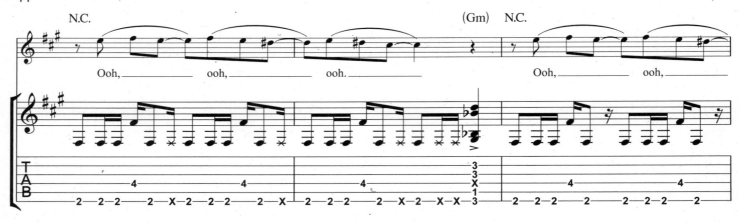

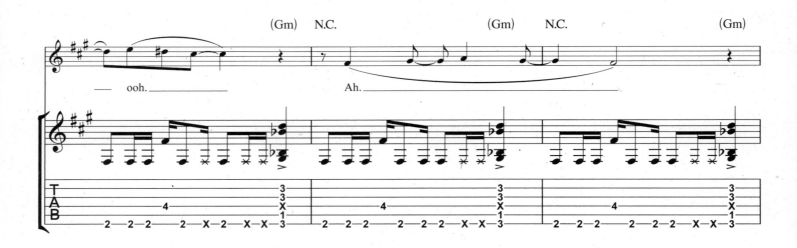

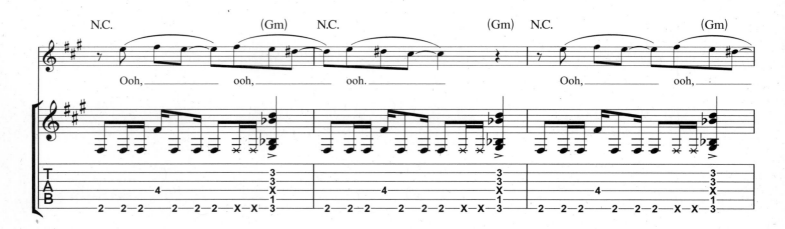

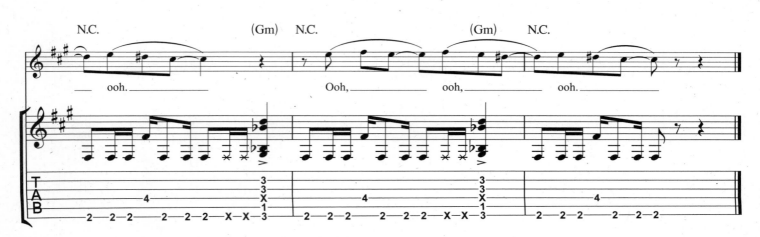

ROCK AND ROLL

Words and Music by
JIMMY PAGE, ROBERT PLANT,
JOHN PAUL JONES and JOHN BONHAM

Rock and Roll - 9 - 1

(A⁵)

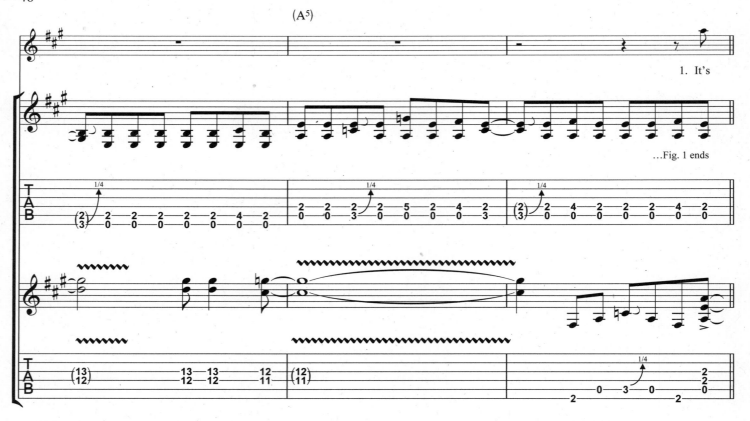

1. It's

...Fig. 1 ends

`00:28; 01:00; 02:24`

𝄋
Verse

(A⁵)

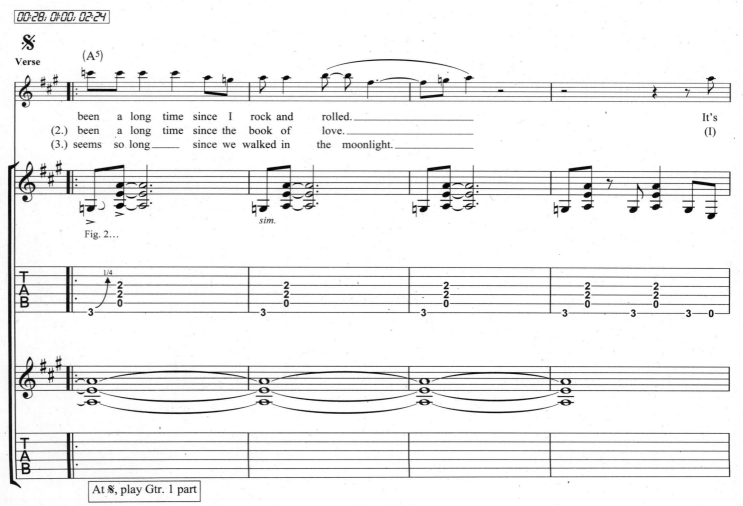

been a long time since I rock and rolled._____ It's
(2.) been a long time since the book of love._____ (I)
(3.) seems so long_____ since we walked in the moonlight._____

Fig. 2...

sim.

At 𝄋, play Gtr. 1 part

48

Play Gtr. 3 part

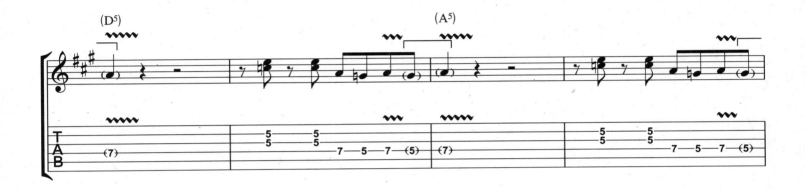

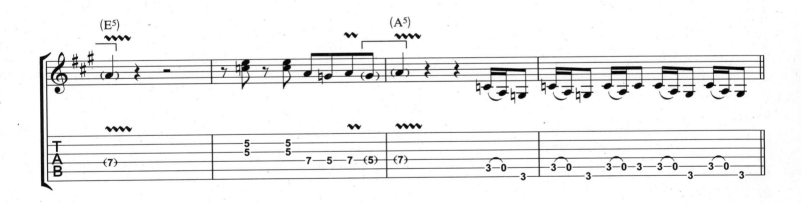

Rock and Roll - 9 - 5

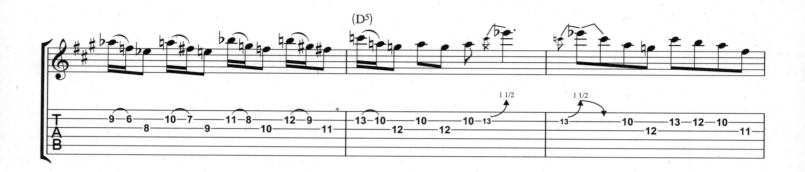

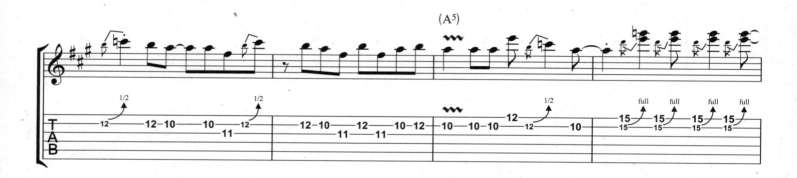

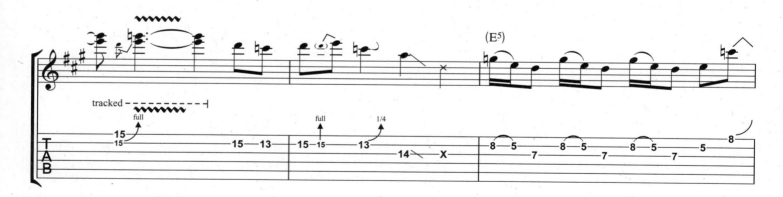

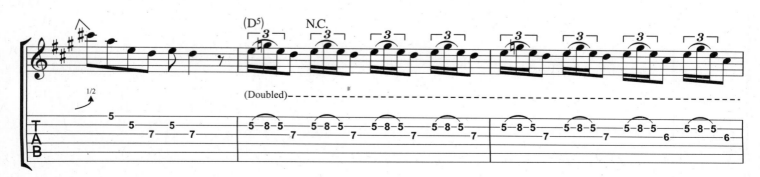

Rock and Roll - 9 - 6

*Regularly played live variant, not performed on original recording

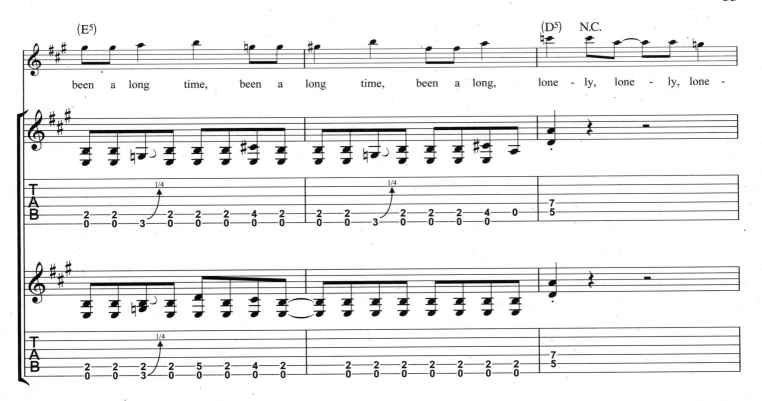

been a long time, been a long time, been a long, lone - ly, lone - ly, lone -

-ly, lone - ly, lone - ly time.

SINCE I'VE BEEN LOVING YOU

Words and Music by
JIMMY PAGE, ROBERT PLANT
and JOHN PAUL JONES

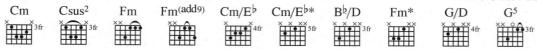

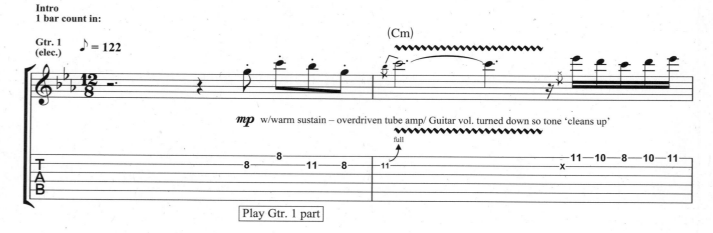

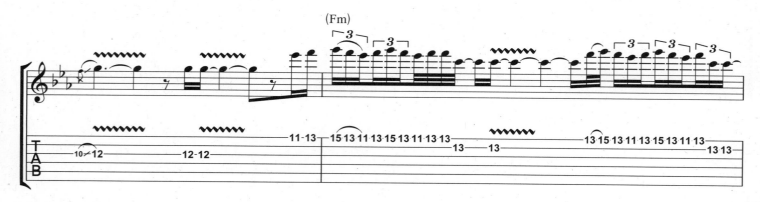

Since I've Been Loving You - 11 - 1

56

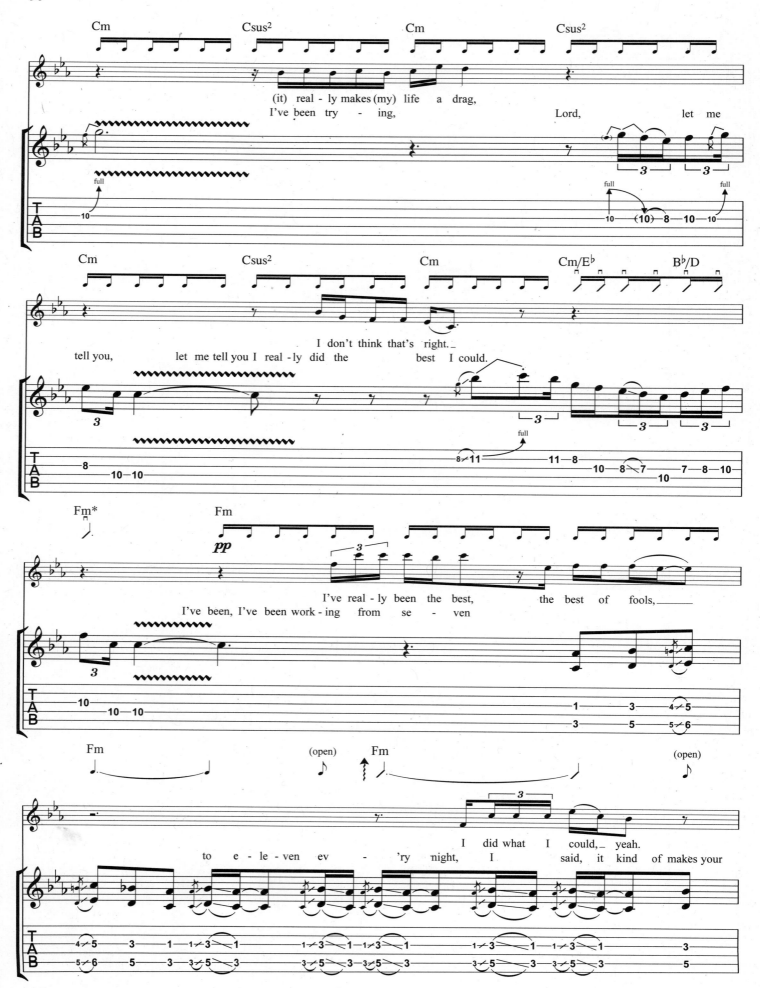

Since I've Been Loving You - 11 - 4

58

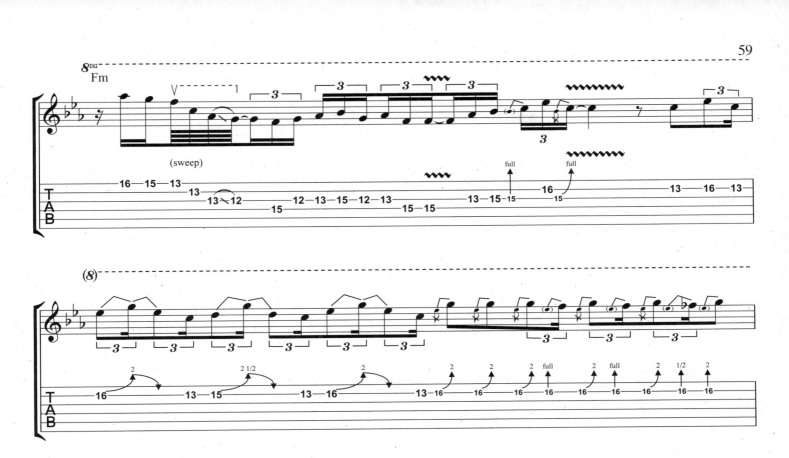

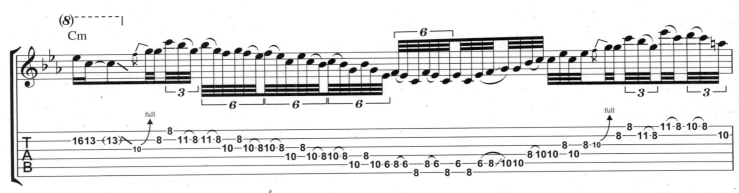

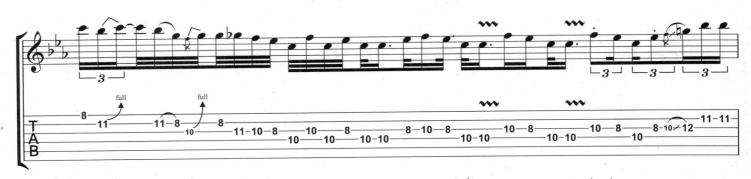

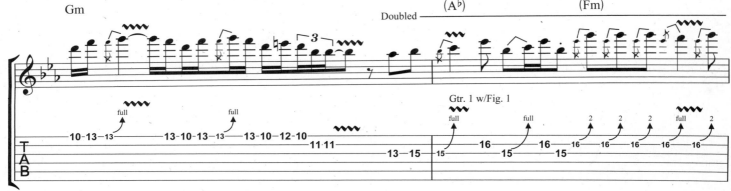

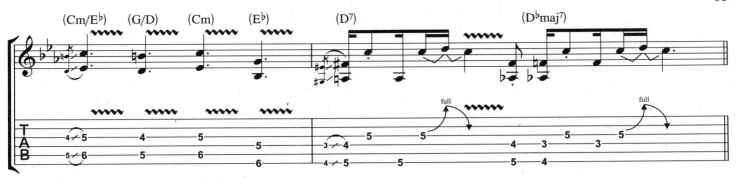

3. Do you re-mem-ber, Ma-ma, when I knocked up-on your door? I said you had the nerve_____

to tell me you did-n't want me no more,_____ yeah._____

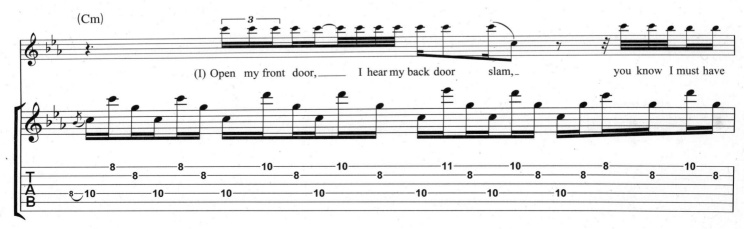

(I) Open my front door,_____ I hear my back door slam,_____ you know I must have

Since I've Been Loving You - 11 - 8

one of them new - fan-gled, new - fan-gled back-door man,_____ yeah, yeah, yeah, yeah yeah.

I've been_ work - ing_ from se - ven, se - ven, se - ven to e -

-le - ven ev - 'ry night, it kind - a makes my life a drag,_

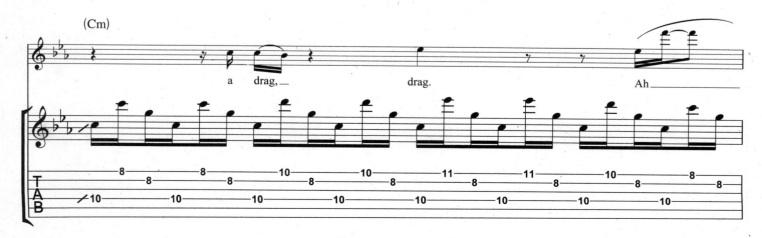

a drag,_ drag. Ah_____

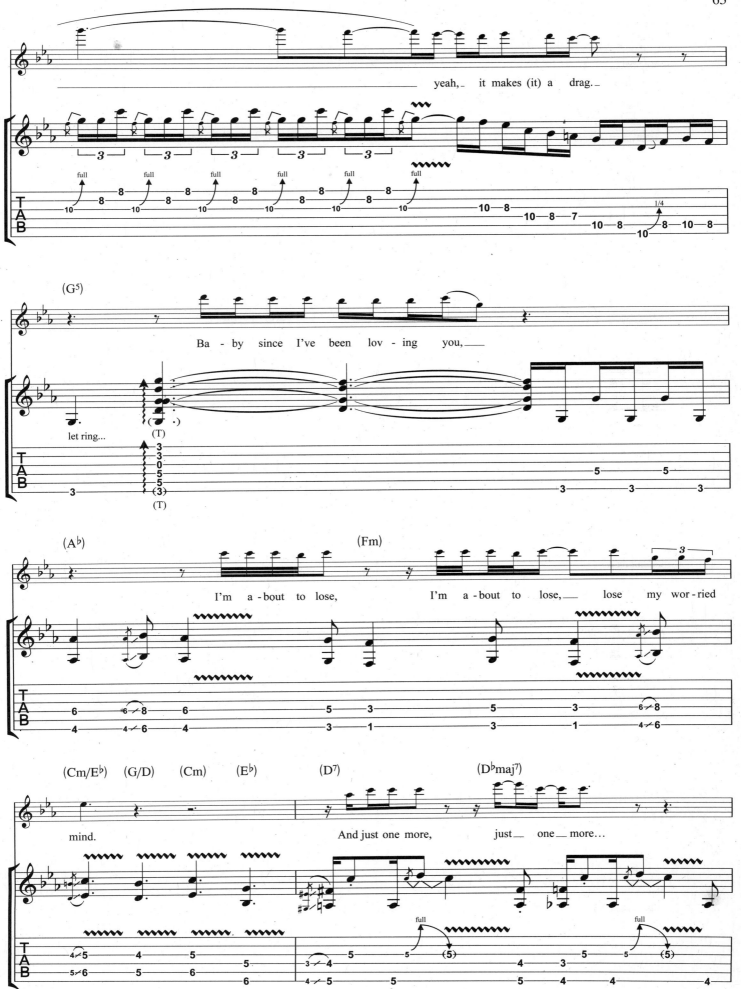

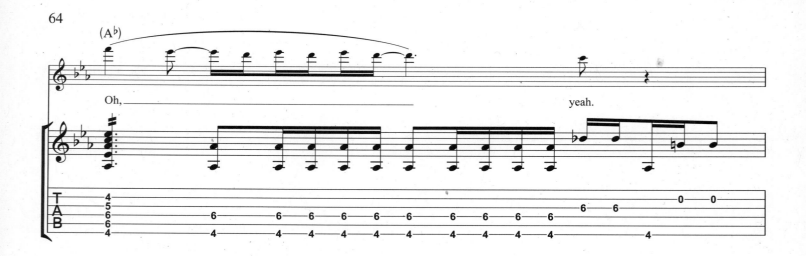

Oh,_____ yeah.

Since I've been lov - ing you, I'm gon - na lose my wor - ried

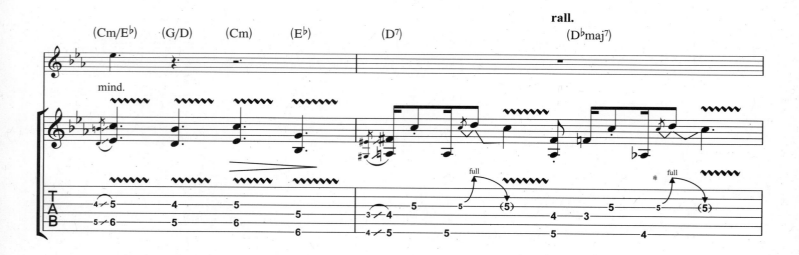

mind.

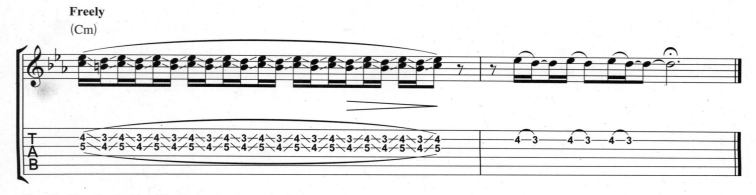

Freely
(Cm)

WHOLE LOTTA LOVE

Words and Music by
JIMMY PAGE, ROBERT PLANT, JOHN PAUL JONES,
JOHN BONHAM and WILLIE DIXON

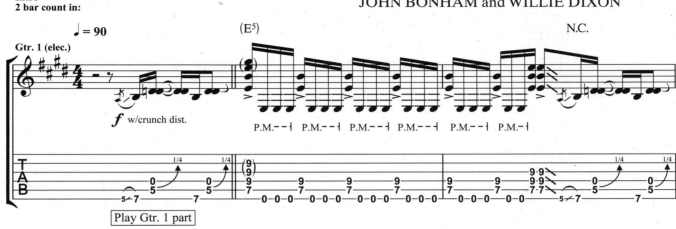

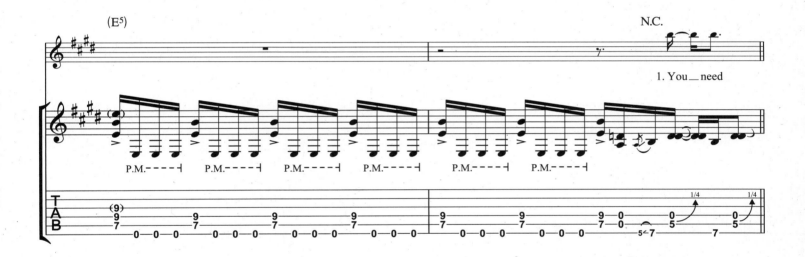

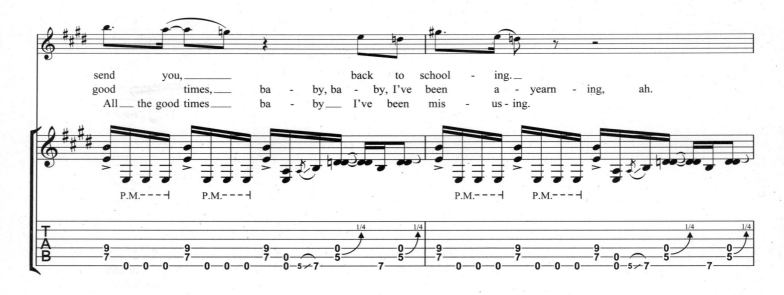

send you,_____   back to school - ing.__
good   times,__ ba — by, ba — by, I've been a - yearn - ing, ah.
All__ the good times__ ba — by__ I've been mis - us - ing.

Way   down in - side,   oh, hon-ey you   need_ it.
Ah, way,   way   down in - side,   oh, hon-ey you   need_ it.
Ah, way,   way   down in - side,   I'm gon-na give you my _ love.

I'm gon-na give you my_ love,_   I'm gon-na give you my_ love.
I'm gon-na give you my_ love,_   ah,_____   I'm gon-na give you my_ love.   Ah._____
I'm gon-na give you ev-'ry inch of   my_ love.____   I'm gon-na give you my_ love.

Whole Lotta Love - 7 - 3

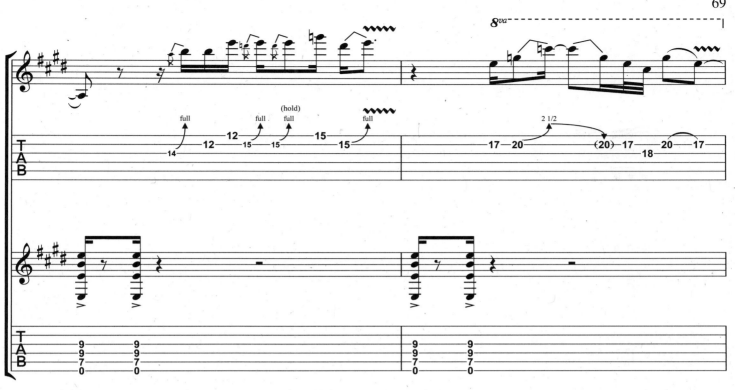

D.S. al Coda

3. You been

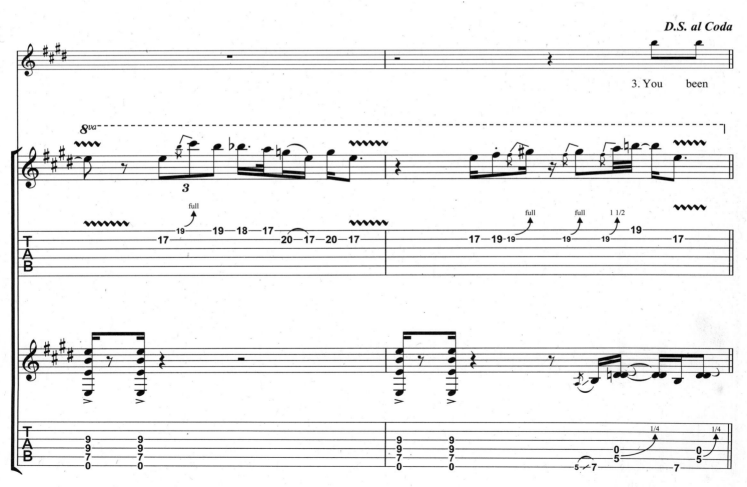

Whole Lotta Love - 7 - 5

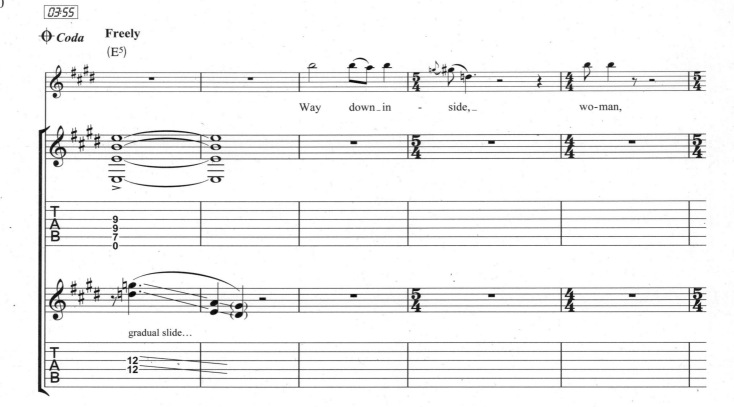

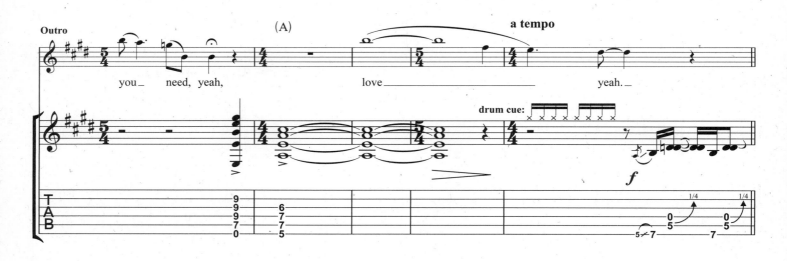

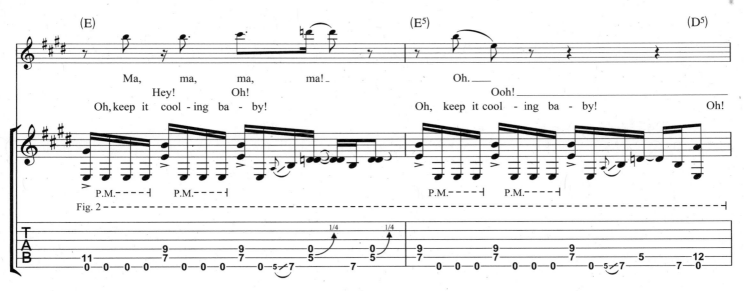

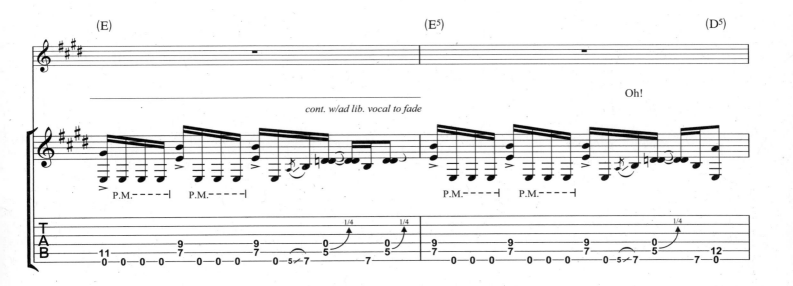

Whole Lotta Love - 7 - 7

GUITAR TABLATURE EXPLAINED

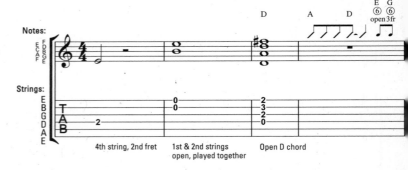

RHYTHM SLASHES are written above the staff.
Strum chords in the rhythm indicated. Round noteheads indicate single notes.

THE MUSIC STAFF shows pitches and rhythms.
It is divided by vertical lines into measures.
Pitches are named after the first seven letters of the alphabet.

TABLATURE graphically represents the guitar fingerboard.
Each horizontal line represents a string and each number represents a fret.

4th string, 2nd fret   1st & 2nd strings open, played together   Open D chord

HALF-STEP BEND:
Strike the note and bend up a half step.

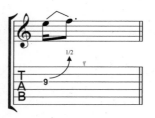

WHOLE-STEP BEND:
Strike the note and bend up a whole step.

GRACE NOTE BEND: Strike the note and bend as indicated. Play the first note as quickly as possible.

QUARTER-STEP BEND:
Strike the note and bend up a 1/4 step.

BEND & RELEASE:
Strike the note and bend up as indicated, then release back to the original note.

COMPOUND BEND & RELEASE:
Strike the note and bend up and down in the rhythm indicated.

PRE-BEND:
Bend the note as indicated, then strike it.

PRE-BEND & RELEASE:
Bend the note as indicated. Strike it and release the note back to the original pitch.

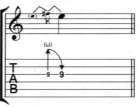

HAMMER-ON: Strike the first note with one finger, then sound the higher note (on the same string) with another finger by fretting it without picking.

PULL-OFF: Place both fingers on the notes to be sounded, strike the first note and, without picking, pull off to sound the lower note.

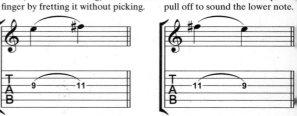

LEGATO SLIDE (GLISS):
Strike the first note and slide the same frethand finger up or down to the second note.

MUFFLED STRINGS: Lay fretting hand across strings without depressing and strike with the pick hand to produce a percussive sound.

NATURAL HARMONIC:
Strike the note while the fret hand lightly touches the string directly over the indicated fret.

PICK SCRAPE:
Rub the edge of the pick down (or up) the string to produce a scratchy sound.

PALM MUTE:
Note is partially muted by the pick hand lightly touching the string(s) before the bridge.

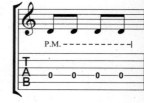

SHIFT SLIDE:
Same as legato slide except the second note is struck.

PINCH HARMONIC:
Simultaneously strike string with pick and flesh of thumb to produce a "squealing" harmonic.

ARTIFICIAL HARMONIC:
The note is fretted normally and a harmonic is produced by adding the pick-hand's index finger at the fret in parens while plucking the string.

TRILL:
Very rapidly alternate between the notes indicated by continuously hammering-on and pulling-off.

RAKE:
Drag the pick across the strings in a single motion.

TREMOLO PICKING:
The note is picked as rapidly and continuously as possible.

ARPEGGIATE: Play the notes of the chord indicated by quickly rolling them from bottom to top.

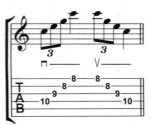

SWEEP PICKING:
Rhythmic downstroke and/or upstroke motion across the strings.

VIBRATO BAR SCOOP:
Depress the bar just before striking the note, then quickly release the bar.

VIBRATO BAR DIP: Strike the note and then immediately drop a specific number of steps, then release back to original pitch